THE BURNING OF

BISHOP NICHOLAS RIDLEY

The Burning of Bishop Nicholas Ridley

Eddie Morales

Illustrated by

Marlon Chang
www.tikkitikki.com

The Burning of Bishop Nicholas Ridley

ISBN 9781938094040

This book is dedicated to

Mr. Frank Ridley

Descendent of Bishop Nicholas Ridley

and

Member of the Meriden Poetry Society
Meriden Public Library
Meriden, Connecticut

Foreword

There exists only two sources of Bishop Nicholas Ridley's life. If there are others I couldn't find them. One source is a digital eBook called *Nicholas Ridley, Bishop and Martyr,* by James Charles Ryle (born May 10, 1816, died June 10, 1900), who was educated at Eton College, Christ Church, Oxford, University of Oxford.

The second source is the book *Nicholas Ridley, A Biography* by Jasper Godwin Ridley (born May 25, 1920 England, United Kingdom, died 2004), educated at the University of Paris, Magdalen College, Oxford. I could find no evidence that Jasper Ridley was at all related to Bishop Nicholas Ridley.

I was able to obtain two copies of this book, one which was sold by a local library to a book store in Philadelphia, Pennsylvania, and the second from a library sold to another local book store in Seattle Washington, both in decent condition. I gave one of the copies to a descendent of Bishop Nicholas Ridley, Mr. Frank Ridley, and the other I kept. Mr. Frank Ridley is, likewise myself, at the writing of this foreword, a member of the Meriden Poetry Society, Meriden, Connecticut, where meetings are held at the Meriden Public Library once a month. It was because of Mr. Frank Ridley that I wrote this poem.

On October 16, 2013, at the Meriden Poetry Society's regularly held meeting, exactly on the 458th anniversary of Bishop Ridley's death, Mr. Frank Ridley expressed the desire to have one of the poets in the group write a poem about Bishop Nicholas Ridley. I decided I would be one of the poets that would write such a poem. Little did I know what I had gotten myself into, and the group didn't realize how seriously I would take this task. The first thing I had to do was find information about Bishop Nicholas Ridley.

Both books mentioned pretty much tell the same story in regards to how Bishop Ridley died. It was not just the fact that Ridley was burned at the stake, but the fact that the ordeal had taken much longer than it should have, and Bishop Ridley's faith in his God never faltered throughout the entire agonizing event.

In brief, to detail what happened to Bishop Ridley, the wood was piled so high, up to his waist, and so thickly packed around him, that when the wood was set ablaze from underneath, the flames could not rise above his waist because there was no room for the flames to pass. As the fire raged, burning him from the waist down, from the waist up it seemed Bishop Ridley could not burn at all. Bishop Latimer, who was burned at the stake alongside Ridley, during their ordeal, would then pronounce the most famous words in all of England:

> *"Be of good comfort, Master Ridley, and*
> *play the man. We shall this day light*
> *such a candle, by God's grace, in England,*
> *as I trust shall never be put out."*

Bishop Ridley would say, among other things:

> *"In manus tuas, Domine, commendo*
> *spiritum meum: Domine, recipe*
> *epiritum meum."*

> "Into your hands, Lord, I commend
> my spirit: Lord, receive my spirit."

These words triggered in my mind the type of poem I would write, the only one I could use, a heroic crown of sonnets.

A heroic crown is an advanced form usually addressed to one person, and/or concerned with a single theme, comprising fifteens sonnets in which the sonnets are linked in the following manner: the last line of the first sonnet is the first line of the second sonnet, the last line of the second sonnet is the first line of the third sonnet, so on and so forth. Then the last sonnet is made up of the first lines of the previous fourteen sonnets, in the exact order presented. So, you really need to write your fifteenth sonnet first, and then write a sonnet for each individual line of the fifteenth sonnet. On top of everything else, the first line of the first sonnet is also the last line of the fourteenth sonnet.

In addition, as a challenge to myself, since each sonnet is fourteen lines long, and the name Nicholas Ridley is exactly fourteen letters long, I decided my fifteenth sonnet, which I would write first, would be an acrostic sonnet. An acrostic sonnet, as with any acrostic poem, uses the first letter of each line to spell a word or message. In this case, the first letter of each line of the sonnet would spell the name of Nicholas Ridley. Now, to the task of writing my fifteenth sonnet first. It took me approximately ten months to write the fifteenth sonnet of my heroic crown, and one month to write the other fourteen sonnets.

Once I had gathered all of the information on Bishop Ridley from the two books, and had written the last sonnet first, an idea occurred to me. The fourteen sonnets reminded me of another series of events about another famous person in religious history. I likened the fourteen sonnets to the *Via Crucis*, also called the *Via Dolorosa* or *Way of Sorrows*, better known as the *Stations of the Cross*. My heroic crown of sonnets was perfect for the poem. The name of this form itself, Heroic Crown, was perfect. The form itself was perfect for relating, sonnet by sonnet, the sequence of events, from Ridley's being declared a heretic, all the way up to his death, the tragedy that occurred in this man's religious lifespan. Then came the next idea to complete my task. As with the fourteen Stations of the Cross, I wanted a visual representation of each phase of the burning at the stake. From the moment Queen Mary declared Ridley and Latimer heretics, all the way to their deaths. I wanted to illustrate the scenes, sonnet by sonnet, as well with pictures, of the burning at the stake of the bishop and martyr, Nicholas Ridley. This heroic crown of sonnets and its illustrations is the result of my acquaintance with the Bishop Nicholas Ridley, who was probably, and maybe still is considered, the most religious man of the Protestant Church, or even of any church. I finished the poem in time for the 459th anniversary of the death of the Bishop Nicholas Ridley. Before you get to the poem, I have provided a timeline of the life of the bishop.

THE

BURNING

OF

BISHOP

NICHOLAS

RIDLEY

*

A HEROIC CROWN OF SONNETS

TIMELINE OF THE LIFE OF
BISHOP NICHOLAS RIDLEY

TIMELINE OF BISHOP RIDLEY'S LIFE

1500

Born in South Tynedale, Northumberland, England, went to Newcastle-on-Tyne for schooling.

1518

He was sent to Pembroke Hall, Cambridge supported by his uncle Dr. Robert Ridley.

1526

Graduated M.A. from Cambridge and went to study at the Sorbonne in Paris and at Louvain, and on his return to Cambridge he was appointed junior treasurer of his college.

1534

He was one of the university proctors, and he signed the decree of the university against the jurisdiction of the pope in England. About this time Ridley, who was now chaplain to the university, began to distinguish himself as an orator and a disputant, and to show leanings to the reformed faith.

1537

Having proceeded B.D., he was appointed by Thomas Cran-
mer, Archbishop of Canterbury, one of his chaplains.

1538

The same prelate instituted him to the vicarage of Herne in
Kent.

1540

He was chosen master of Pembroke Hall.

1541

He became chaplain to King Henry VIII and canon of Canter-
bury.

1543

He was accused of heretical teaching and practices, but he man-
aged to allay the suspicions of the royal commissioners, alt-
hough just after his exculpation he finally abandoned the

doctrine of transubstantiation.

1547

Ridley was presented by his college to the Cambridgeshire living of Soham, and in September of the same year he was nominated Bishop of Rochester. King Edward VI was now on the throne and the new bishop was in high favor. He was one of the visitors who were appointed to establish Protestantism in the University of Cambridge.

1548

He helped to compile the English prayer book.

1549

He was one of the commissioners who examined Bishops Gardiner and Bonner. He concurred in their deprivation and succeeded Bonner in the see of London.

1553

Having signed the letters patent settling the English crown on Lady Jane Grey, Ridley, in a sermon preached at St. Paul's cross on the 9th of July 1553, affirmed that the princesses Mary and

Elizabeth were illegitimate and that the succession of the former would be disastrous to the religious interests of England. When Lady Jane's cause was lost, however, he went to Framlingham to ask Queen Mary's pardon, but at once he was arrested and sent to the Tower of London. From his prison he wrote in defense of his religious opinions.

1554

He, with Cranmer and Latimer, was sent to Oxford to be examined. He defended himself against a number of divines, but was declared a heretic, and this was followed by his excommunication. He refused to recant.

1555

October 16, he was tried for heresy under the new penal laws, being degraded and sentenced to death. He was burned at the stake

A HEROIC CROWN FOR THE

BISHOP NICHOLAS RIDLEY

RIDLEY AND LATIMER ACCUSED OF HERESY

SONNET I

North of the city, in fair Oxford town,

The word was out where all could come to see

The execution of one of their own,

A man of the cloth: Nicholas Ridley.

His faith in God was his only defense,

However, Mary, crown without pardon,

Took all his beliefs to heart and offense,

And had him arrested, well and anon.

The method chosen, to burn at the stake,

Befit the cruelty Bloody Mary sought

To vanquish her enemies, swiftly break

The Reformation, by all deeds and thought.

The decree to burn would carry her threat,

In a ditch, one near Balliol College set.

RIDLEY AND LATIMER ARE TAKEN TO THE STAKE

SONNET II

In a ditch, one near Balliol College set

The stage was readied for the pyre of wood,

The timber high, stacked too much to forget,

Like some fair symbol of a holy rood.

The lord Williams, by the Queenly command,

In fear of the tumult that might arise,

Was made to assist, put soldiers at hand,

To assure the prisoners their demise.

When all was in readiness to proceed,

The mayor, bailiffs, by the laws then writ,

Brought forth the captives, as was so decreed,

And placed them in that unbearable pit.

So, there stood the man, in fair and black gown,

Called Bishop Ridley, ordered by the Crown.

RIDLEY KISSES THE STAKE HE WILL BE BURNED AT

SONNET III

Called Bishop Ridley, ordered by the crown,

Stood he with Master Latimer as well,

To walk into the pit, before the town,

They both made ready for the flames of hell.

In God they trusted to assuage the fire,

Or Lord give strength to help withstand the pain

That would no doubt consume them in the pyre,

In hopes their souls His Heaven's Kingdom gain.

"Be of good heart," said Ridley to his friend,

Whereat, serenely, went he to the stake

And kneeled before it, knowing well the end

Was near, and kissed it for his goodly sake.

No pardon from the queen, her mind was set,

Heresy charged, to burn his pious debt.

RIDLEY AND LATIMER WHISPER TO EACH OTHER

SONNET IV

Heresy charged, to burn his pious debt,

Unshaken his faith, prayed Ridley to God.

He knew in his heart He'd not soon forget

To free his soul of its earthly façade.

By his friend kneeled Latimer, and joined in

To ask the Lord for the same, to be freed.

They'd soon be rewarded for failure to sin,

In their gravest and direst hour of need.

They arose and spoke so no one could hear,

And what was said could be learned of no man,

As if it were said for only God's ear,

So left they all to the Lord's master plan,

The wood to be placed, around and around,

On, from waist to feet, wood so tightly bound.

RIDLEY GIVES TIPPET AND GOWN TO SHIPSIDE

SONNET V

On, from waist to feet, wood so tightly bound

Would prove to Ridley he would burn the worst.

Ahead, Ridley took his tippet and gown

And gave them both to Master Shipside first.

Preacher Smith's sermon went unanswered, for

The crowd was so forbidden to reply.

Whatever else was given out before

The wood was placed, and not one eye was dry.

Happy he who might get rags from Ridley,

Or reach with slightest touch his flesh exposed,

For Ridley wanted so his God to see,

That of all there, he was the most composed.

Well Ridley knew the time, it swiftly came,

Lit the fire, he'd not flee his heavy frame.

RIDLEY ACCEPTS THE BAG OF GUNPOWDER

SONNET VI

Lit the fire, he'd not flee his heavy frame,

The wood around him so heavy and tight,

As if his legs and the wood were the same,

Where struggling by far was a hopeless plight.

Around Ridley's waist the smith wrapped a chain;

Took Master Latimer same iron belt,

And both took the gunpowder, bagged and plain

Around their necks, where the flesh may melt.

Still, Ridley took this from God as a sign

That all was heaven and blessedly sent,

His life there given, a decree divine,

Once the end delivered, his life all spent.

Yet, Ridley prayed England's safety abound,

Against the torch, the agonizing sound.

THE PILE OF WOOD IS LIT FROM BELOW

SONNET VII

Against the torch, the agonizing sound,

At Ridley's feet, a wood kindled with fire

Was placed to catch the rest that wrapped around,

While he wished his death be Heaven's desire.

No room existed for the flames to rise,

The raging inferno trapped in the wood,

His flesh in turmoil, unseen by all eyes,

And Master Latimer spoke, "Be of good

'Comfort, Master Ridley, and play the man.

'We shall this day light such a candle, by

'God's grace, in England, as I trust shall

'Never be put out." Then the fire drew nigh;

And Ridley, ready, the closer it came,

Stoically, he withstood the hellish flame.

BISHOP RIDLEY PRAYS TO THE LORD

SONNET VIII

Stoically, he withstood the hellish flame,

While all who witnessed remembered him when

This man from South Tynedale, thrown on to pain,

By villainous crown, and deceitful men,

Veered not from his faith, sought all that was good,

In honesty, in godly trade, his life

Upon the honored path, as all men should,

And women pure, despite whatever strife

May come; who took all things upon his heart,

With malice none, nor rancorous intent,

So gave he prayer and contemplative part

For he thought all on earth heavenly sent.

In England, not in Rome, nor anywhere,

Righteous more than Ridley, none could compare.

BISHOP RIDLEY BEGS THE LORD FOR MERCY

SONNET IX

Righteous more than Ridley, none could compare,

Nothing but godliness reigned in him still,

And though he was just, the scene was unfair,

And left he to God the whole of his will.

The fire raged on, kept down by the wood,

And he wished, by the pain, it would take him

Away; but more of the agony would

He come to endure, most dreadful and grim.

"Lord have mercy upon me," was his cry.

In all his torment, he didn't forget

His Savior and Lord, who knew how to die

For greater sins the world would beget.

He showed Queen Mary, and the world, that day,

In faith and deed, from the Lord he'd not stray.

BISHOP LATIMER IS THE FIRST TO DIE

SONNET X

In faith and deed, from the Lord he'd not stray,

His holy persuasion would see him through

The agony of the flesh dealt that day,

As higher and higher the set fire grew.

"Oh, Lord, Lord, receive my spirit!" He cried.

Latimer followed, "Father of heaven,

'Receive my soul!" And then Latimer died

Leaving Ridley there yet to be taken.

Oh, to die for one's faith and conviction!

This is the tragedy here in detail—

To find at the stake one's own affliction,

Like Son on the Cross with hammer and nail.

"Lord!" Yelled Ridley, into the smoky air,

Dauntless, unfailing, for end to despair.

BISHOP RIDLEY STATES HE CANNOT BURN

SONNET XI

Dauntless, unfailing, to end the despair,

"Lord have mercy upon me," came his plea.

"Let the fire come unto me," was his prayer,

For more wood had been stacked, and all could see

Greater torment it caused upon his face.

"I cannot burn!" he said, writhing in pain,

Asking for mercy and God's saving grace,

Said over and over this sad refrain.

His turmoil, whereof he had no release,

Engaged the crowd and the multitudes wept,

All vehemently praying God grant him peace,

And send him to where all good souls are kept.

Ridley craved the end, to see Heaven's way,

(Latimer by his side), without delay.

A BYSTANDER PULLS OFF TOPMOST WOOD

SONNET XII

Latimer by his side, without delay,

A thought to a man in the crowd occurred,

To use his bill to pull the wood away,

And took to action with nary a word.

He pulled off the topmost bundle of wood,

And the flames leapt higher from that one side.

Then Ridley, seeing this, enough withstood,

Wrested himself to the fire, and then died

When the gunpowder blew over his face.

Master Ridley was seen to stir no more,

His soul moved on to a happier place,

Where God, before him, opened Heaven's door.

At last it had come, the end of his life,

Ever swiftly, by Death, healer of strife.

RIDLEY FINALLY SUCCUMBS TO THE FLAMES

SONNET XIII

Ever swiftly, by Death, healer of strife,

Our man of the cloth was sadly taken

Away, away, away to a place of no grief,

Unto the Lord for faith not forsaken.

In silence, but for the sobs and the tears,

All looked on to what was left of the man,

Nicholas Ridley, and offered their prayers

For him to rise to the heavenly span.

Too quickly do good men live well and die,

While evil ones do ill and live too long,

Which begs all faithless souls to wonder why,

While faithful ones know here's where they belong.

Like from the tree that gives, the last, its leaf,

Yielded Ridley, to God, all of his life.

ALL MOURN BISHOP NICHOLAS RIDLEY'S DEATH

SONNET XIV

Yielded Ridley, to God, all of his life.

No man of history could give much more.

No man could boast his faithful callings rife

With saintly grace, which leads to God's own door.

What queen and country could not nobly give,

The flames gave well, his flesh to be consumed,

And by his name, good Bishop Ridley, live

Within the vault of martyrdom entombed.

There were signs of woefulness on all sides,

The loss of all the earth now Heaven's gain,

But weep not, for God's hand has reach and guides

The faithful to be free of woe and pain.

There ends the story of martyr and crown,

North of the city, in fair Oxford town.

BISHOP NICHOLAS RIDLEY

SONNET XV

North of the city, in fair Oxford town,

In a ditch, one near Balliol College set,

Called Bishop Ridley, ordered by the crown,

Heresy charged, to burn his pious debt.

On, from waist to feet, wood so tightly bound,

Lit the fire, he'd not flee his heavy frame.

Against the torch, the agonizing sound,

Stoically, he withstood the hellish flame.

Righteous more than Ridley, none could compare,

In faith and deed, from the Lord he'd not stray.

Dauntless, unfailing, to end the despair,

Latimer by his side, without delay,

Ever swiftly, by Death, healer of strife,

Yielded Ridley, to God, the last of his life.

THE END

OTHER BOOKS BY THE AUTHOR

A Reason for Rhyme

The Suicide Sonnets

Count Edweird Lefang's Rhymin' Halloween

A Candle on Fire

Poems for Edna

For the Love of Nine Muses

Made in the USA
Las Vegas, NV
08 May 2025

21880538R00030